BUILDINGS
OF THE WORLD

Created by olo.éditions
www.oloeditions.com
115, rue d'Aboukir
75002 Paris
France

EDITORIAL CONCEPTION
Nicolas Marçais

DESIGN CONCEPTION
Philippe Marchand

EDITORIAL
Claire Tréboute
Diane Routex

AUTHOR
Emmanuelle Graffin

ENGLISH-LANGUAGE EDITION

EDITORIAL
Christopher Westhorp

TRANSLATION
James Hodgson

Cover credits: (right) ©Simon Bond/Getty;
(left) ©Robert Essel/Corbis, ©Atlantide Phototravel/Corbis,
©Philip Wegener/Beateworks/Corbis.

ISBN: 978-2-9532483-6-4

British Library/Library of
Congress line

Date of printing: August 2011
Printed in Singapore
by Tien Wah Press

BUILDINGS OF THE WORLD

75 ARCHITECTURAL WONDERS THAT AMAZE, INSPIRE, AND INTRIGUE

INTRODUCTION

Buildings of the World presents 75 of the boldest, most extraordinary structures of the last 20 years. By undertaking this survey of contemporary architecture, the book aims to identify current and future trends in building design. Vying with each other for our attention, these spectacular buildings are testament to the pressures exerted on architects by the cultural and economic forces of our day.

Buildings of the World acquaints—or perhaps reacquaints—you with the works of internationally renowned architects such as Jean Nouvel, creator of the Agbar Tower in Spain, and Zaha Hadid, who conceived the enigmatic Phaeno Scientific Center in Germany. And there's a chance to venture into the world of the Swiss agency Herzog & de Meuron, designers of the famous "Bird's Nest" National Stadium built for the 2008 Beijing Olympics. The book also celebrates the work of less well known, but equally creative agencies, such as Future Systems, whose groundbreaking Investec Media Centre stands over the Lord's cricket ground in London, and WilkinsonEyre, designers of the ingenious Gateshead Millennium Bridge in Newcastle. Care has been taken to include the widest possible variety of buildings—museums, concert halls, retail stores, skyscrapers, company head offices, apartment blocks, places of worship, libraries...—constructed in the widest, most innovative range of materials, from concrete, glass, steel, aluminum, and titanium to plastics, composites, and even reclaimed shipping containers.

Inviting you on a veritable voyage of architectural discovery and opening a window onto a world of innovation and creativity, *Buildings of the World* is, above all, a celebration of diversity and uniqueness.

SELFRIDGES
BIRMINGHAM, UK

With its bionic architecture inspired by natural forms, this branch of the famous British department store Selfridges has completely revitalized the centre of Britain's second city.

For the company's Birmingham branch, the head of Selfridges wanted an ultra-modern building that would contrast strongly with its neoclassical store on London's Oxford Street. Having been impressed by its space-age design for the Investec Media Centre at Lord's cricket ground (see pages 192–193), he commissioned the cutting-edge British agency Future Systems. Opened to the public in 2003, the entirely bubble-shaped structure follows the natural contours of the site. The building is covered in 15,000 discs of spun aluminum, an idea that came from a famous metal-plated dress by the French couturier Paco Rabanne. The surface below the discs has been painted royal blue to set them off. Inside, the space is defined by an immense, organically shaped atrium, with escalators carved out of the void. Natural light flows through the roof. Described as "blobitecture" (architecture using organic, gentle, or rounded forms), this building can be put in the same bracket as Peter Cook's art gallery in Graz (see pages 20–23).

ESPLANADE—THEATRES ON THE BAY
SINGAPORE, SINGAPORE

Dominating the surrounding landscape, these two armadillo-like shells are the defining features of the Esplanade arts complex, one of Singapore's major attractions.

The Singapore practice DP Architects collaborated with the British agency Michael Wilford & Partners to produce this gigantic cultural center, which opened in 2002. Located on a 15-acre site on Marina Bay, next to the historical and administrative district and close to the mouth of the Singapore River, the building comprises two enormous, organically shaped shells. These structures are each supported by a three-dimensional steel framework entirely covered in glass. The architects wanted people inside the buildings to enjoy a stunning, panoramic view over the city and for the theaters to be equally striking to people viewing them from the outside, but they also needed to shield occupants from the intense tropical sun. Their solution was to cover the glass shells in triangular sunshades, each of which is angled in such a way as to offer maximum protection without compromising views. The complex includes a 1,600-seat concert hall, a 2,000-seat theater, an opera house, an outdoor performance space, restaurants, a shopping center, and a major arts library.

CITY OF ARTS AND SCIENCES
VALENCIA, SPAIN

Organized around three themes (the arts, the sciences, and nature), this gigantic, futuristic complex has become a favorite destination for both Spanish and international visitors.

The City of Arts and Sciences is a cultural complex set on an 86-acre green space on the outskirts of Valencia, the birthplace of its architect, Santiago Calatrava. Construction work lasted more than ten years (1998–2009), but the end result was a spectacular variety of buildings: L'Hemisfèric (a planetarium and IMAX movie theater); the Museu de les Ciències Príncipe Felipe (a science museum); L'Umbracle (a long, arcaded glasshouse containing a botanical gardens and promenade); L'Oceanogràfic (a giant aquarium designed by the architect Félix Candela); the Palau de les Arts Reina Sofía (a boat-shaped opera house); and L'Àgora (a vast covered plaza). But it is L'Hemisfèric and the Museu de les Ciències that stand out as the development's most iconic structures. For the former, Calatrava took inspiration from the anatomy of an eye, with the planetarium as the eyeball held in a three-dimensional concrete socket that opens and closes like an eyelid. In contrast, the science museum resembles a concrete and glass dinosaur skeleton.

TOKYO BIG SIGHT
TOKYO, JAPAN

With its unique, monumental design and its arresting public artworks by world-famous artists such as Claes Oldenburg, this exhibition and convention center is highly prized by locals and tourists alike.

Produced in 1996 by the Japanese agency AXS Satow Inc., this major convention center is located on the artificial island of Odaiba in Tokyo Bay. The most visually striking part of the complex, the Conference Tower, consists of four upturned pyramids each supported by a glass tower. This eight-story concrete-and-steel structure stands 190 feet tall and is clad in aluminum and glass. It holds a 1,100-seat convention room, as well as other smaller conference facilities on its various levels. There are also two exhibition spaces, the East and West exhibition halls. The East Exhibition Hall features a 2,000-feet long, two-tier gallery. This is covered by an enormous glass roof, which is equipped with an electronic sunshield system to regulate the entry of natural light. The West Exhibition Hall consists of four halls around a central, two-level atrium. The complex also boasts numerous restaurants, and various outdoor exhibition spaces overlooking the bay.

SEATTLE CENTRAL LIBRARY
SEATTLE, USA

Dubbed the "Library for All," this astonishing structure, endorsed by the public but criticized by architecture correspondents, was partly financed by Bill Gates.

The inhabitants of the city of Seattle campaigned for a new city-center library to replace two existing ones that have since been demolished. The winners of the competition to design the new library were the Dutch architect Rem Koolhaas's OMA (Office for Metropolitan Architecture), in association with the Seattle practice LMN Architects. Opened in 2004, the building fulfills the classic functions of a library as well as housing an auditorium, a car park, and various annexes. The 184-foot high steel and glass construction has a distinctive prismatic form, which stems from the shape of the interior spaces. Inside, readers can enjoy amazing views over the city and Elliott Bay. A four-story space called the Books Spiral houses the library's non-fiction collection. Despite a highly controversial design, this library has been a clear success with the public.

ORIENTAL PEARL TV TOWER
SHANGHAI, CHINA

Looking like something straight out of a science-fiction movie, the "Oriental Pearl," as it has become known, is famous throughout the world and attracts more than three million visitors each year.

The 1,535-foot TV and radio tower stands on the edge of the Huangpu River in the Lujiazui business quarter in Pudong, Shanghai. This strikingly original structure was built in 1995 by the Chinese architect Jia Huan Cheng. Supported by sturdy angled pillars, the tower is articulated by 11 spheres of various sizes, which are linked by concrete columns. Clad in metal, these balls shine in the sky, and reflect in the river, like precious pearls—an important symbol in Chinese culture. The building rises up from an area of luxuriant vegetation, which some poetic souls have likened to a jade plateau. The tower boasts a host of attractions: a revolving panoramic restaurant at 876 feet from ground level, observation decks at 863 and 1,148 feet, a nightclub, numerous shops, conference facilities, a hotel, and a huge underground wax museum devoted to the history of Shanghai.

This social housing project, located in a middle-class area, "looks like a giant display of potted plants ... and [is] one of the best places to live in Paris," according to an article in the *Guardian* newspaper.

The French architect Édouard François, who designed this 2004 building, is a fervent believer in green architecture and sustainable urban planning. The design he submitted to his client, a construction company specializing in social housing, consisted of a ten-story building containing 30 residences and an indoor car park, which would be covered in plants all year round. Some 380 concrete pots were planted with bamboos, which, growing to an average height of 13 feet, provide the occupants with a degree of privacy and shade. There is a sophisticated irrigation system to keep the plants watered and healthy: rainwater is collected in an underground tank where it is enriched with fertilizer before being redistributed to the balconies by means of an automatic spray.

100 11ᵀᴴ AVENUE
NEW YORK, USA

With its windows set at a multitude of angles to capture the light as it changes throughout the day and the year, this abstract composition, or "vision machine," reflects the liveliness of the neighborhood in which it is situated.

Occupying a prime piece of Chelsea real estate, the corner of 11th Avenue and West 19th Street, this 22-story apartment block was designed by the French architect Jean Nouvel. Completed in 2010, it contains luxury apartments that enjoy a perfect view over the Hudson River. Keen to make the most of the building's river-facing side, the architect proposed a curtain-wall of a complexity unprecedented anywhere in the world. It consists of a patchwork of 1,750 square and rectangular windows in 32 different sizes, each of which is set at a different angle. Some of them open, others are fixed. This façade is made up of "megapanels" prefabricated in China, each of which comprises several windows and constitutes the external wall of one room. In contrast, the rear façade, which faces toward Midtown Manhattan, is composed of black brickwork perforated by openings of different sizes, set at different angles.

JEAN-MARIE TJIBAOU CULTURAL CENTRE
NOUMÉA, NEW CALEDONIA

The air-circulation system means "the huts emit a particular noise, a sound, almost a voice," explains the architect. "It's the sound of Kanak villages, their forests, of a sea port on a windy day."

Located to the north of Nouméa, on a peninsula stretching out into Magenta Bay, the building is heavily inspired by Kanak culture, which was the intention of its Italian architect Renzo Piano. For this project he worked with an ethnologist who had specialist knowledge of the Kanak people. Dedicated to the independence campaigner Jean-Marie Tjibaou, who was assassinated in 1989, the building is organized around ten huts strung along a central covered path—a typical Kanak village layout. The huts come in three different sizes and vie with the tall, thin pine trees that one finds everywhere on the island. The structures were designed to resist cyclones—a frequent occurrence in tropical regions—and earthquakes. The architect has used stainless steel and iroko, an African wood that is extremely moisture resistant and which, over time, takes on a silvery patina identical to that of the palm trees that are also common on the island. The air-circulation system is achieved by means of a double wall, which, as well as offering acoustic benefits, also provides natural ventilation.

ALLIANZ ARENA
MUNICH, GERMANY

Designed for the 2006 FIFA World Cup, and nicknamed the "Schlauchboot" (rubber dinghy), this fantastic stadium is particularly impressive at night, when it is lit up and changes color.

The Swiss architects Herzog & de Meuron have a way of surprising with their innovative and original design solutions. In this case, they covered a prefabricated concrete structure in an envelope of 2,874 lozenge-shaped air cushions, which are kept inflated by a constant flow of air. The cushions are made of ETFE (see page 16), a very durable material, which is also fire resistant and recyclable. Thanks to an electronic fluorescent lighting system, these panels can change color according to the team that is playing at the stadium: white for the national team, blue for TSV 1860 Munich and red for Bayern Munich. What's more, the cushions are transparent, so they allow natural light to pass through them, which helps keep the pitch in good condition. Opened in 2005, the stadium is located to the north of the city center and has a capacity of 66,000 spectators. The highly technical nature of the design led to a substantial construction budget, much of which was met by the insurance company Allianz, which gave its name to the stadium.

ORIENTAL ART CENTER
SHANGHAI, CHINA

Enigmatic by day, when it is hidden behind curved glass façades that repel the gaze of curious onlookers with a reflection of Shanghai, this building becomes more forthcoming at night, when it is lit up to reveal the richness of its interior spaces.

Set in the heart of Pudong, on a confined site nestling between Century Avenue and nearby parkland, this enormous cultural complex was produced in 2004 by the French architect Paul Andreu. The seven-story, steel and laminated-glass building is most notable for its distinctive shape: viewed from above, it resembles a flower comprising five petals of different sizes all joined together under the same roof. Each petal contains a large hall (namely, the entrance hall, the Performance Hall, the Concert Hall, the Exhibition Hall, and the Opera Hall) and is connected to the others via the middle of the flower, which acts as a kind of central dissemination zone. The building also features music stores, a restaurant, and an arts information center. As an aid to navigation, the various spaces are differentiated by their layout and their color scheme, but, taking their cue from the exterior spaces, they all evoke the organic forms of nature.

OPÉRA DE LYON
LYON, FRANCE

Playing with harmonies of black, red, and gold, transparency and opacity, contrasting materials and qualities of light, the architect has succeeded in his aim of making this opera house the "beating heart of the city."

Located in the centre of Lyon, on the Place de la Comédie, between the Rhône River and the city hall, this project by French architect Jean Nouvel, completed in 1993, is an extension of the existing neoclassical Chenavard and Pollet opera house, which dates from 1831. From the original building, only the façades and the foyer have been retained. Nouvel has topped the structure with a steel-and-glass barrel vault, which has doubled the height of the original building. This vault consists of a series of semicircular arches, lacquered light gray, which support an initial layer of glass covered in a silkscreened-glass sunshield. The audience enters from the Place de la Comédie, through the peristyle that extends along three sides of the building. Inside, there are 18 levels, of which the bottom five are below ground and the top six are housed within the glass vault. The building comprises a 1,100-seat opera house, rehearsal rooms, a 200-seat amphitheater, administrative offices, workshops, and a restaurant. The main auditorium is lined in dark wood with touches of gold.

PETRONAS TOWERS
KUALA LUMPUR, MALAYSIA

Opened in 1998, these twin towers were the tallest buildings in the world until the construction of Taipei 101 in 2004.

Designed for Petronas (the Malaysian national oil company) by the American architect César Pelli, the towers stand out because of their huge size. They are joined together between the 41st and 42nd floors by a 190-foot long suspension bridge. The buildings are made from high-strength concrete. The façades are covered in a steel-and-glass curtain wall and feature stainless-steel sunscreens to protect occupants from the intense tropical sunlight. The exteriors convey motifs from Islamic art in an act of homage to Malaysia's official religion. In another reference to Islamic art, the ground plans of the towers consist of two squares superimposed on each other to form an eight-pointed star. Alternating rounded and squared projections create a jagged façade. Each story has 22,000 square feet of free floor space. The towers contain not only offices, but also more than 10 million square feet of shops and leisure facilities, a concert hall, a mosque, a multimedia conference center, and a bowling alley.

K OF CHINA
G KONG, CHINA

j Shui experts sionately criticized tower for its sharp, ressive edges, ing the architect ctantly to modify his gn.

igned by the American itect I.M. Pei, and ring service in 1990, ower was built for Bank of China. It ains to this day one of g Kong's most iconic scrapers. The building ,000 feet tall and its masts, which reach a ght of 1,204 feet, made e tallest skyscraper in g Kong for a number of rs, until it was deposed he International mmerce Centre, One Two International ance Centre and ntral Plaza. It has 72 rs and 14 million are feet of office space. metal latticework the reflective-glass ain walls are distinctive ures of the façade. The ding is composed of asymmetric vertical ments, which build on top of the other l they finish in a single ngular prism. Thrusting nto the sky, the cture is reminiscent bamboo, an Asian bol of prosperity longevity. In China, buildings have to be igned in consultation a Feng Shui master, he American architect's cision to go it alone sed a great scandal.

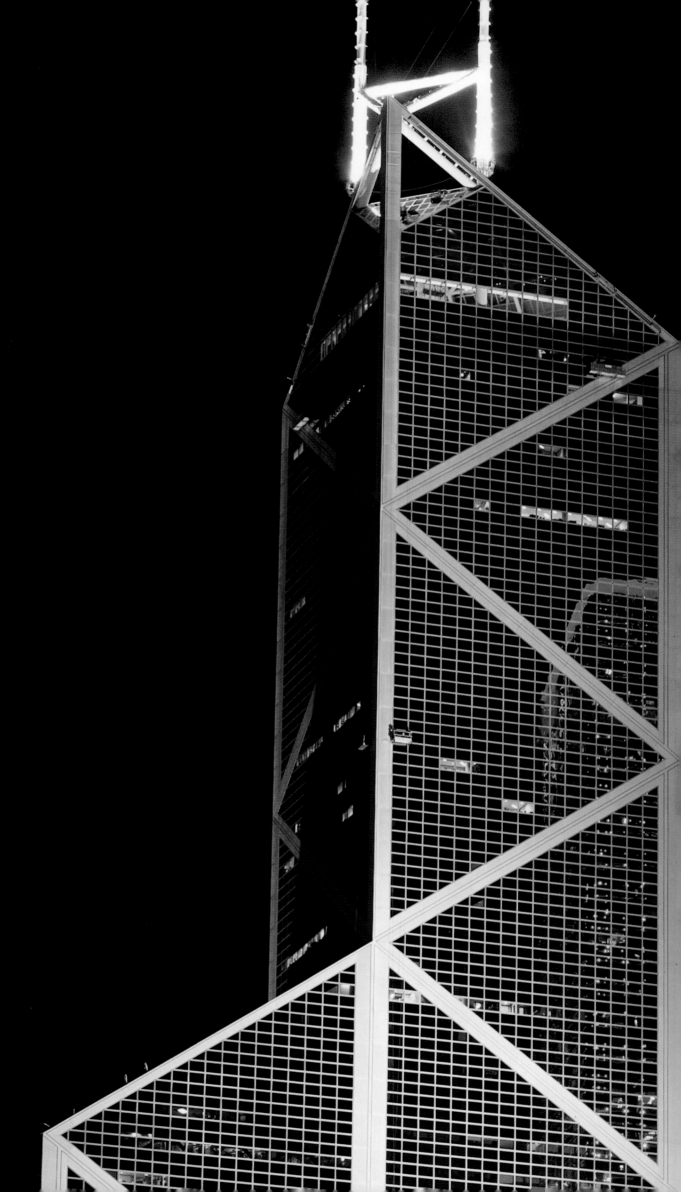

OKYO CITY HALL
KYO, JAPAN

e profile of its façade ings to mind a gothic thedral—particularly tre Dame in Paris, hich the architect ted as an influence.

ompleted in 1991, the uilding is the work of panese architect Kenzo nge. It is situated in the hinjuku business district, nd consists of two entical 797-foot towers, hich are joined together om the base all the way o to their 33rd floors. The wers contain the city overnor's office, municipal fices, conference halls, a saster prevention center, nd offices for various her public bodies. he upper parts of the wers get progressively arrower. There is a public bservation deck on the 5th floor, from which, on good day, you can see lount Fuji in the distance. he skyscraper was esigned in accordance ith Japan's stringent arthquake-damage mitation regulations. This stantly recognizable uilding imposes itself n the urban landscape— deed, it used to be the ity's tallest until it was vertaken by Midtown ower (813 feet).

NGDOM CENTRE
YADH, SAUDI ARABIA

rince Alwaleed,
randson of the founder
' Saudi Arabia, King
bdul Aziz, wanted to
uild a tower that would
e as representative of
s country as the Eiffel
ower is of France.

ompleted in 2002,
e building was jointly
roduced by the American
gency Ellerbe Becket and
e Saudi Arabian Omrania
Associates. It is instantly
entifiable by the upturned
arabolic arch at its top,
elow which there are
fices, a hotel, apartments,
nd the headquarters of a
ank. On the three bottom
oors of the building you
ill find a shopping mall, a
ports center, conference
alls, and an enormous
ar park. At 1,050
et, this is the tallest
kyscraper in Riyadh.
nother distinguishing
eature is that its upper
nd lower sections were
uilt completely differently:
e base section is made
ut of reinforced concrete,
hereas the upper portion
s built with metal girders.
s in the case of most
igh-rise buildings, there
s an observation deck at
e top. The curtain-wall
çade made of reflective
lue glass contributes
o the imposing effect of
e building, which has
ecome a symbol of Saudi
rabian economic might.

AGBAR TOWER
BARCELONA, SPAIN

Opened by the king of Spain in 2005, and nicknamed the "suppository" by the local population, this skyscraper has provoked fierce controversy because of its phallic contribution to the Barcelona skyline.

Standing 466 feet tall, and topped with a huge metal-and-glass dome, the Torre Agbar (in Catalan) dominates the city from its position near the Plaça de les Glòries Catalanes. This bullet-shaped building, designed by Jean Nouvel, looks as if it has burst out of a water-filled crater. The external framework is concrete and is supported by a slightly offset central cylinder. All this is hidden behind a casing made of small strips of colored glass on a coated steel surface. The overall effect is one of fuzziness: "… it's a fluid mass that seems to spurt out of the ground, like a geyser at a constant and controlled pressure," explains the architect. The construction project proved to be particularly testing. Because of the poor soil quality, the foundations had to be dug almost 150 feet deep, and the shape of the tower itself and its architectural refinements also presented countless technical challenges.

JIN MAO TOWER
SHANGHAI, CHINA

Like many Asian buildings, the Jin Mao's proportions derive from the number eight. An auspicious number in China, eight symbolizes wealth and prosperity.

Rising to a height of 1,380 feet, the 88-story Jin Mao Tower ("golden prosperity building" in Chinese) was completed in 1998. It was produced by Skidmore, Owings & Merrill (SOM), a world-leading specialist in high-rise architecture. Located in the Pudong district of Shanghai, the tower symbolizes China's new-found status as an economic superpower. Taking its cues from traditional Chinese architecture, particularly the pagoda, the Jin Mao is gradually stepped back as the building rises. The refinement of the materials—chrome, granite, glass—and some of the detailing refers back to existing buildings of the region. For example, the 160-foot curtain-walled pinnacle echoes the form of the lotus flower of Shanghai. Built to withstand typhoons and earthquakes, the tower consists of office space up to the 50th floor, with the upper part of the building reserved for a five-star, 550-room hotel, the highest in the world. In common with many other skyscrapers, the top two floors house a panoramic restaurant and an observation gallery offering breathtaking views over the city. A dizzying, 33-story atrium has been hollowed out of the center of the building.

BURJ KHALIFA
DUBAI, UNITED ARAB
EMIRATES

Inspired by Arabian culture allied with cutting-edge technology, Burj Khalifa is currently the world's tallest building at 2,716 feet.

Designed by the American agency Skidmore, Owings & Merrill (SOM) and opened in January 2010, Burj Khalifa is to form the centerpiece of a new district, "Downtown Dubai," located to the south of the historical heart of Dubai. The area will comprise a 30-acre artificial lake, 30,000 dwellings, nine hotels, at least 19 apartment blocks, the world's biggest shopping mall, and 7.5 acres of parkland. The tower has 160 habitable floors, taken up by apartments, office space, and a luxury hotel. The total budget of the Burj Khalifa project has reached approximately one billion euros. This steel and glass minaret can be seen from a distance of 60 miles. Its construction has required 11.65 million cubic feet of concrete and 34,600 tons of steel. A total of eight escalators and 57 lifts have been installed to move people up and down the building. The unprecedented scale of this project is testimony to the reckless property development taking place in the emirate of Dubai, which has narrowly avoided bankruptcy.

TURNING TORSO
MALMÖ, SWEDEN

It was an architect-produced sculpture called "Turning Torso," consisting of nine marble cubes connected by a spinal column, that inspired this 623-foot tower. It is the tallest building in Scandinavia and the second tallest in Europe.

Designed by Santiago Calatrava, Turning Torso opened in 2005. Built in a new residential district of Malmö, the tower is on the banks of the Øresund Strait and looks across to Copenhagen. It is made up of nine irregular pentagonal blocks, each one five storys high. Offices occupy the first two blocks; apartments, the seven others. The blocks pivot in a clockwise spiral around a central axis, the spinal column of the building, so that the top block is at 90 degrees in relation to the bottom one. This creates a twisted effect that seems to defy gravity. The core part is made of concrete and the external structure, which is metal, stabilizes the building against high winds. The curtain walls are encased in glass and metal. "I try to break down the boundaries between architecture and sculpture and to perceive architecture as art," comments Calatrava to explain this spectacular, sculptural tower, which contrasts so strongly with the surrounding landscape. This design takes us back to the Renaissance, when artists were painters, sculptors, and architects all at the same time.

PRADA AOYAMA EPICENTER
TOKYO, JAPAN

After the success of its flagship New York store designed by Rem Koolhaas, the famous fashion company Prada enlisted the highly creative Swiss architects Herzog & de Meuron to produce their Tokyo showcase.

Finished in 2003, the shop is in the heart of Aoyama, the haute couture capital of Tokyo. Everything about this six-story building dazzles with its inventiveness. It has five faces and resembles a child's drawing of a house. Its surface looks as if it has been cut like a diamond: lozenge-shaped glass panels, all of which are transparent except the ones for the fitting rooms, which are translucent, bring the façades to life. The development incorporates a plaza with a small moss garden in the shelter of a wall—an unusual use of space in a city in which every last square inch is built on. The lattice of steel tubes gives structure to the exterior and supports the building. From the inside these tubes are white and are set off by an array of textures: pony skin, silicon, fiberglass, oak … The whole design serves as a luxurious showcase for the clothes on display.

CASA DA MÚSICA
PORTO, PORTUGAL

Designed to be the home of the Porto Philharmonic Orchestra, this many-sided "House of Music" is an amazing example of architecture as contemporary sculpture.

Designed by the architects Ellen van Loon and Rem Koolhaas and the Office for Metropolitan Architecture, the Casa da Música was intended as the emblem of Porto's year as European Capital of Culture in 2001. However, it was only completed four years later, in 2005. The building is a 180-foot high polyhedron built on a travertine plaza opposite the Rotunda da Boavista, one of the city's major traffic intersections. The white concrete shell holds the main concert hall, which can accommodate an audience of 1,300. At each end, corrugated glass allows in natural light while also enhancing the acoustics of the space. In another measure to improve the acoustics, the interior of the hall is lined with plywood embellished with gold leaf. The plan oblique view of the base of the building takes in the shape of the two additional auditoriums. The architect wanted the building to be one of the city's treasures, so he took particular pains to make the white concrete façade as smooth as possible by incorporating an aggregate of local granite.

CALTRANS DISTRICT 7 HEADQUARTERS
LOS ANGELES, USA

Tearing up all the norms of office-building design, this kinetic construction, inspired by the world of the automobile, is reminiscent of a freeway.

This futuristic new regional headquarters for the state transportation agency Caltrans was created by the American practice Morphosis. Handed over in 2004, the building is in downtown Los Angeles, opposite the city hall. Designed to accommodate 2,500 office workers, a café, a parking garage, a daycare center, and conference facilities, the structure is organized into two main elements: one with 13 levels and another, which is perpendicular to the other, that has four levels. A central hall connects the two elements. Inside the building, the offices are laid out along the façades in open, flexible spaces, so that they receive as much natural light as possible. The exposed galvanized-steel framework is clad in perforated-aluminum panels, which can be opened and closed automatically to regulate the entry of sunlight during the day. When they are opened at night, the façade of the building is completely transformed. The horizontal and vertical circulation spaces have been carefully planned to promote social interaction between employees.

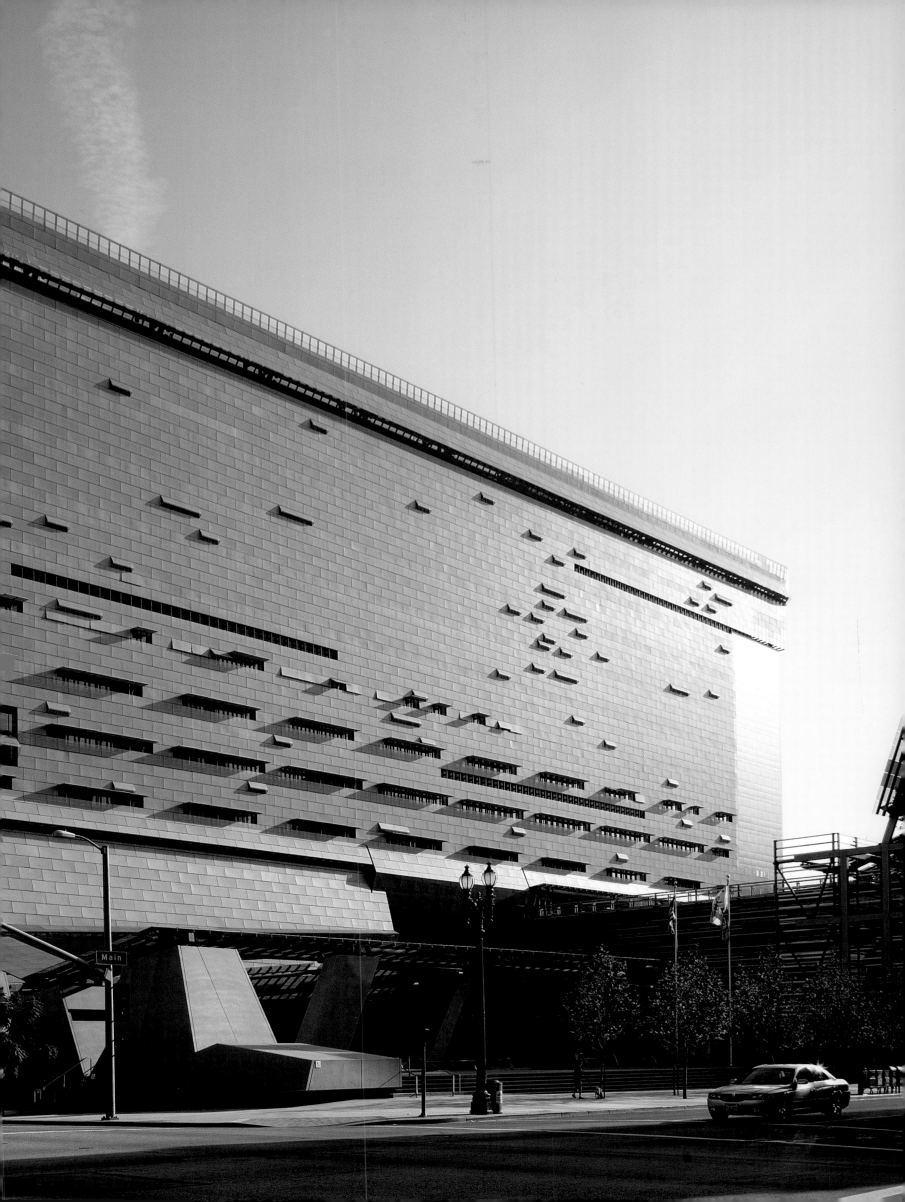

WHITE TEMPLE
KYOTO, JAPAN

This modern sanctuary, displaying a typically Japanese simplicity, is used mainly for funeral ceremonies and the honoring of ancestors.

Built in 2000, the temple was designed by the Japanese architect Takashi Yamaguchi. It is located northeast of Kyoto, in a peaceful spot surrounded by lush vegetation and close to a lake—ideal for meditation and contemplation. Its architecture is dramatically different from that of the traditional Buddhist temple next to it. The building consists of a massive rectangular block of concrete painted an immaculate white. This whiteness contrasts strongly with the black gravel surface that surrounds the building— and makes it look as if the temple has just been placed on the ground. The interior contains two sections separated by a stepped marble platform, which takes up most of the room: one of the areas is for the relatives of the deceased, whereas the other houses memorial tablets. The architect took particular pains over the subdued light coming through the window on the rear wall and the frosted-glass skylights that run along the sides, because he wanted the interior to change according to the intensity of the light outside.

SCHAULAGER
BASEL, SWITZERLAND

The Schaulager, or "viewing warehouse," is a new kind of museum. A genuine one-of-a-kind, it acts both as a storage facility for the works of more than 150 artists and as an exhibition space.

Custodians of a sizable collection of modern and contemporary art, the Emanuel Hoffmann Foundation engaged Herzog & de Meuron to design a building that would incorporate a warehouse, an exhibition space, and a research center. Situated on the outskirts of Basel and completed in 2003, the structure is notable for the simplicity of its regular, cuboid form and the coarseness of its façade, an effect achieved by mixing concrete with an aggregate material derived from excavation works. Completely opaque, apart from a jagged horizontal incision along some of the façade, the building blends into its surroundings, as if it had been extracted from the ground during an archeological dig. One of the exterior walls is indented to create a covered entry plaza sheltering a small gatehouse, which has been rendered in the same type of concrete as the main building. Inside, an atrium provides a glimpse of the museum's five floors: the bottom two floors are given over to permanent and temporary exhibitions; the top three floors are reserved for storage.

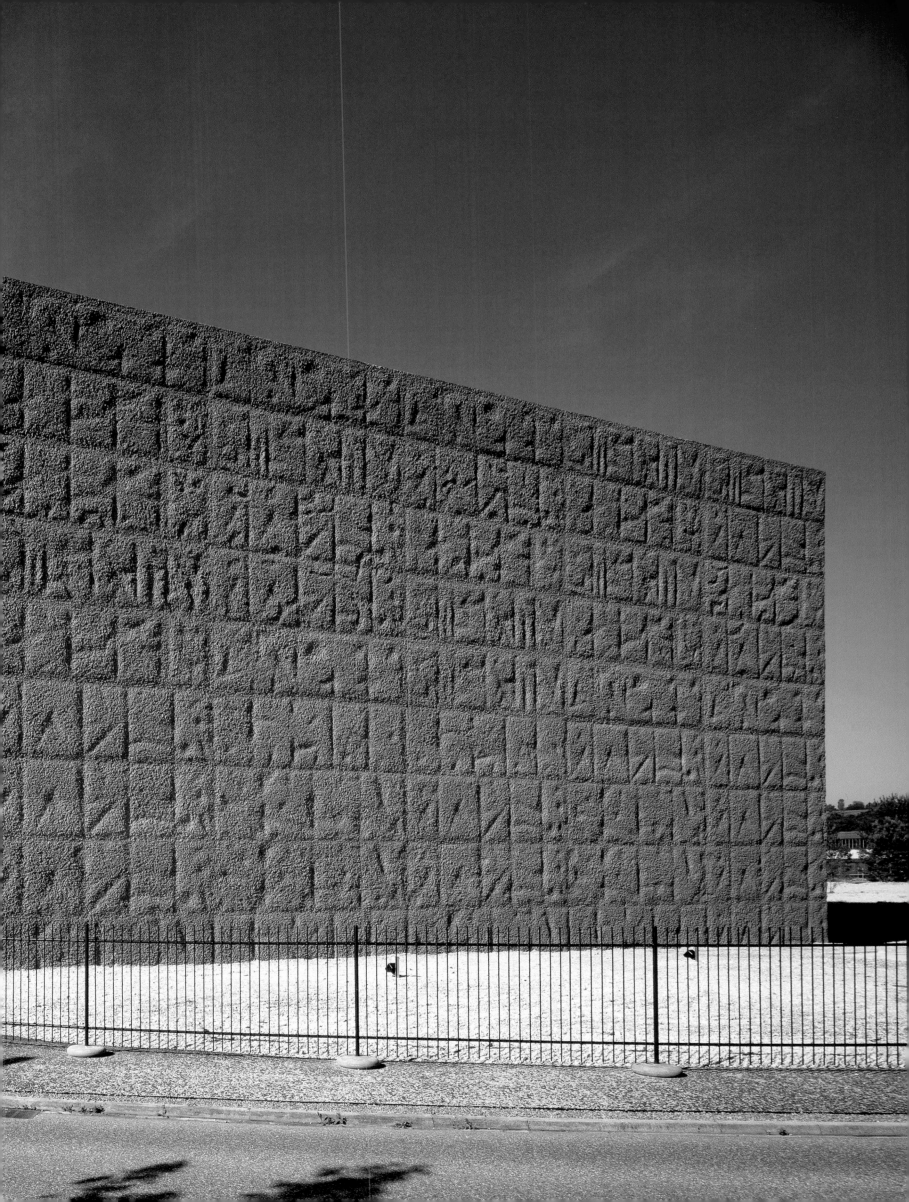

MODERN ART MUSEUM OF FORT WORTH
FORT WORTH, USA

With light playing on concrete, glass, and water, this museum sparkles against the night sky. The reflections in the pool that surrounds it accentuate the magical effect of its restrained, elegant design.

The stakes were high for the Japanese architect Tadao Ando, renowned as a great exponent of concrete: his work would stand opposite one of the most famous museums of the 20th century, the Kimbell Art Museum, built in 1972 by the American Louis I. Kahn, another master manipulator of concrete. Far from being inhibited, Ando has made a statement of his own. Completed in 2002, the museum is in Fort Worth's outskirts, on a vast green space with an artificial lake. The two museums are separated by a wooded parking lot. Ando's museum consists of a row of five two-story rectangular boxes, the three smallest of which contain the exhibition spaces. The concrete frameworks are encased in glass to allow natural light to enter the interior. The only concrete elements to appear on the exterior of these glass pavilions are the Y-shaped pillars that support the cantilevered roofs. In the words of Ando: "I ... wished to attempt a dialogue with Kahn, and thereby extract a spatial essence comprising a strong simplicity and clarity with which to imbue the new building."

MICHAEL LEE-CHIN CRYSTAL, ROYAL ONTARIO MUSEUM
TORONTO, CANADA

Taking the name of its main benefactor, the Michael Lee-Chin Crystal has revitalized the image of the Royal Ontario Museum, Canada's principal museum of natural history and world cultures.

This extension to the 1912 museum was opened in 2007. Located on the corner of Queen's Street and Bloor Street (one of Toronto's main shopping thoroughfares), the design by Polish–American architect Daniel Libeskind sits neatly along the side of the original neoclassical building, but then spills out over the street in a series of spectacular cantilevers, one of which provides the new entrance to the museum. The architect's brief was to renovate ten existing galleries and design a new building to house an underground exhibition hall, six new galleries, restaurants, offices, and a gift shop. The metal structure is made up of five prismatic shards, which fit together to create vast atriums. The building is clad in brushed aluminum, except for where it has been lacerated to form window openings, which make up 25 percent of the façade and carry natural light into the interior.

-AHILL CENTER
ASADENA, USA

n keeping with its role
s an astronomical
bservatory, this
uilding is pierced by
glass-roofed vertical
olume, which not only
onveys natural light to
he interior but enables
tar-gazing.

Conceived by Morphosis
nd completed in
2008, the center forms
art of the California
nstitute of Technology
Caltech), an organization
enowned as a pioneer
n space observation and
xploration. The building
vas designed to unite
nder a single roof a dozen
r so research teams
reviously scattered across
Caltech's South Campus.
ocated on the northern
dge of the South Campus
nd directly opposite
he North Campus, the
enter provides a link
etween the university's
vo campuses. The
tructure has a distinctive
ense of movement—a
Morphosis trademark—
et it blends in perfectly
vith its environment:
s scale, orientation,
orizontal massing, and
uilding materials echo
he Spanish-tinged
rchitecture of the
urrounding buildings. The
outhern façade opens
nto an expanse of athletic
elds edged with newly
lanted sycamore groves,
vhich form a natural
oundary as specified
y the designers. More
nclosed, the northern
açade overlooks the
istoric core of the campus
nd, in the distance, the
San Gabriel Mountains.

The winged structure on top of this station, located close to Lyon, brings to mind a majestic bird preparing to take off.

Renowned for his delicate, airy works of art, the Spaniard Santiago Calatrava designed this rail station using the very latest construction techniques. The station, which entered service in 1994, comprises five high-speed train platforms, each 1,300 feet long. The two central tracks, known as the "tube 300," are isolated from the rest and enable trains to travel through the station, without stopping, at nearly 200 mph. The building is topped with a curved concrete, steel, and glass structure, which runs perpendicular to the tracks and measures almost 1,000 feet long by 130 feet high. A long footbridge containing a moving walkway links the station to the neighboring Saint-Exupéry international airport. Even with such a breathtakingly monumental and original design, the station is underused—partly because it is difficult to reach from the center of Lyon and partly because the airport hosts relatively few long-haul flights.

AKRON ART MUSEUM
AKRON, USA

This futuristic museum building is notable for its chaotic, fragmented form, which stands in the city like a three-dimensional signpost.

Coop Himmelb(l)au, an Austrian agency renowned for its deconstructivist designs, produced this extension for the art museum in Akron, Ohio, in 2007. The building is organized around three strongly defined elements. The "Crystal," a flexible space, marks out the main entrance and links the extension to the original museum. Immediately recognizable from the outside by its dramatic, sloping glass wall, it hosts exhibitions and performances and allows access to the other areas. Next, the "Gallery Box" contains a vast exhibition space. Finally, the cantilevered armature known as the "Roof Cloud" gently floats on top of the rest of the structure. While still allowing natural light to enter, it shelters the interior from the sun's strongest rays, and throws shade onto the street below. Its horizontal profile functions as a dramatic local landmark. The complex serves not just as a museum, but as an urban space—visitors come to "hang out" or to attend performances, wandering seamlessly between the exterior and the interior.

UMEDA SKY BUILDING
OSAKA, JAPAN

From the moment of its construction, this skyscraper became Osaka's landmark building. It is a prime example of the modernity of the city, which had to be completely rebuilt after its bombardment in the Second World War.

Built in 1993, this totally futuristic structure was conceived as a three-dimensional city by the Japanese architect Hiroshi Hara. Standing next to the Yodo River in the downtown Umeda business and shopping district, the building consists of two separate 567-foot towers. These are connected by various bridges, panoramic elevators, and escalators, which criss-cross the empty space in between. Topping the whole structure is a platform with a large circular hole in the center, which makes the building resemble a launch pad. This floating city houses restaurants whose décor was inspired by picturesque Japanese streets, as well as a public observation deck affording breathtaking views over the city and its river. The three-dimensional elements of the structure were assembled on the ground during building works and then lifted up into position.

MILWAUKEE ART MUSEUM
MILWAUKEE, USA

The museum's new wing has helped to give a strong identity to a building that was lacking in personality, and has turned Milwaukee into an unmissable cultural destination.

This work by Santiago Calatrava, famed for his white, airy designs, takes its inspiration from the natural world. The building has restructured and reinvigorated the original museum, designed by the Finnish architect Eero Saarinen in 1957. Produced in 2001 on the banks of Lake Michigan, this was Calatrava's first commission in the USA. It is dominated by the enormous sunscreen that stands out against the sky. Composed of 72 pairs of white steel fins operated by hydraulic cylinders, this structure opens and closes like the wings of a majestic bird. It shelters an elliptic entrance hall topped with a sloping glass ceiling. From here, visitors can access the various exhibition galleries, both new and old, as well as the war memorial, an existing feature of the original museum. On the outside, a 250-foot long suspended footbridge, supported by an angled mast and cable stays, opens up the museum to the rest of Milwaukee by linking it to the city's main shopping street.

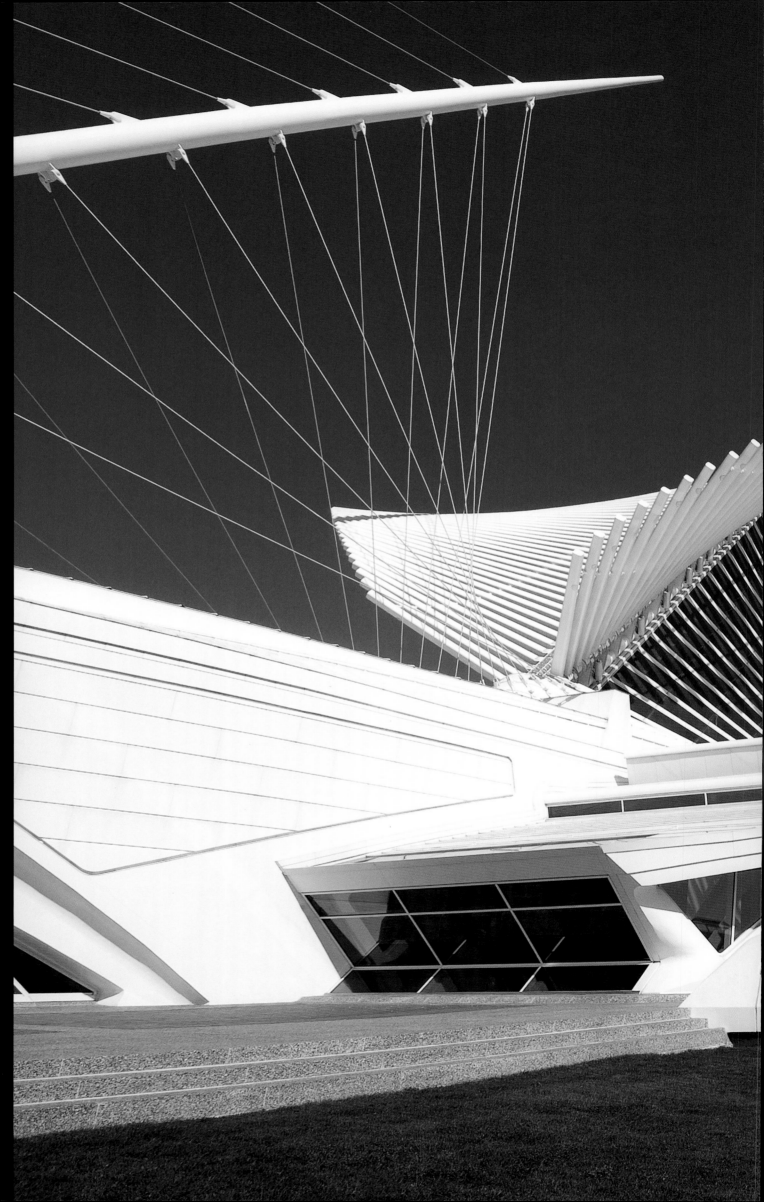

WEISMAN ART MUSEUM
MINNEAPOLIS, USA

Resembling a waterfall or even an abstracted fish, this museum has met with approval from visitors and architecture critics alike. Indeed, a *New York Times* reviewer described it as having "five of the most gorgeous galleries on earth."

Part of the University of Minnesota, this privately funded museum is the work of the Canadian–American architect Frank Gehry. Completed in 1993, the building stands between the Washington Avenue Bridge to the north and the Coffman Memorial Plaza to the south, and offers stunning views over the Mississippi. The four-story structure contains stock rooms, shops, offices, and exhibition galleries, which are laid out in a large cuboid volume at the southeast corner. The main entrance can be reached via a footbridge that crosses over the Washington Avenue Bridge. The styles of the different sides of the building contrast strongly. The rear façade, which faces the university campus, is in brick, so that the museum blends in with its brick- and stone-built neighbors. However, on the other side the building presents an intricate arrangement of overlapping scrolls clad in brushed-steel panels and interspersed with a large number of window openings.

THE ALUMINIUM CENTRE
HOUTEN, THE NETHERLANDS

This aluminum building on stilts seems to be alive, like a forest of poplars bent by the wind—a typical feature of the Dutch landscape and one that inspired this project.

The young Dutch architect Micha de Haas produced this unusual construction on the sloping banks of a lake in Houten on the outskirts of Utrecht. The structure, built to host conferences and meetings for the aluminum industry, serves as an advertisement of the metal's qualities. Completed in 2001, the building consists of a simple box held up by a thick crop of 368 randomly positioned stilts. These aluminum tubes are approximately 52 feet high and some of them are curved. The architect drew on aerospace technology for some aspects of the design. The aluminum theme even runs to the pebbles on the banks of the water, which are made out of bauxite, the ore from which the metal is extracted. The complexity of the lower part of the structure is in complete contrast to the simplicity of the upper part, which is also made from aluminum.

INFRONT HOSPITALITY
LUSTENAU, AUSTRIA

Situated in the middle of a field in a rapidly expanding retail park, this building was designed in part to advertise the company it houses, and it also acts as a striking landmark against its rural backdrop.

This minimalist oblong box was built in 2000 by the Austrian architect Dietrich Untertrifaller. Commissioned by an events management company, the building (originally known as Walch's Event Catering) contains storage and production facilities, offices, and a small apartment. It took only a year to build—a record time! Its framework is made out of prefabricated wood and the interior and exterior walls are in OSB (oriented strand board), a composite wood product made out of long strips of wood fiber that is currently in vogue among architects. The Austrian artist Peter Kogler produced the outer layer, using a textile imprinted with tubular shapes—this creates a kind of watery effect and enables occupants to see out from the inside without being seen from the outside. This fabric covers the whole structure, disguising both the form and the function

BARAJAS AIRPORT TERMINAL 4
MADRID, SPAIN

Recognizable by its colorful, wavy design, this new terminal has increased the capacity of Barajas Airport from 20 million to 70 million passengers a year, making it one of Europe's busiest.

Jointly conceived by the British agency Richard Rogers Partnership and the Spanish practice Estudio Lamela, this high-tech terminal building was opened in 2006. Its prefabricated-steel roof, resembling a rippling wave, is the most distinctive feature of the design. The roof sits on top of a concrete framework and is supported by Y-shaped steel girders, called "trees" by the architects, which are painted in a gradation of colors stretching out over 1,000 yards. Perforated with openings that convey natural light to the passenger concourse on the upper level, the interior surface of the roof is clad in bamboo strips to provide a sense of warmth. Color is used systematically to designate different zones and to help passengers trace the progression of the spaces. As a further demarcation measure, the main passenger-processing areas are separated by long stretches of light wells, called "canyons," which also diffuse natural light throughout the different levels of the terminal. On the outside, the curtain-wall façade is equipped with louvered shading to shield the interior from the most intense sunlight.

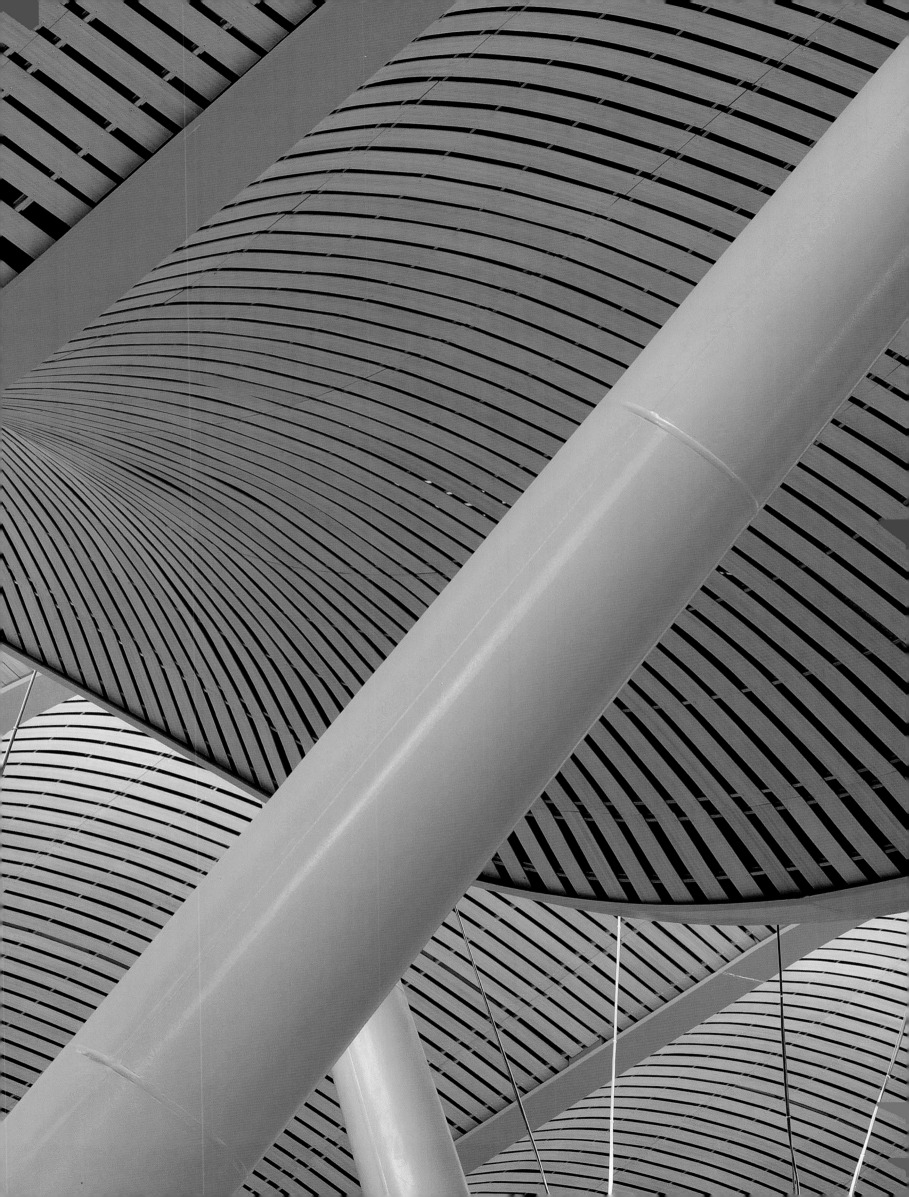

ST MARY AXE
LONDON, UK

Nicknamed the "Gherkin," this office block has become a true London landmark and a model of environmental design known throughout Europe.

Opened in 2004 and designed by Sir Norman Foster, the structure has permanently altered the skyline of the City, London's business district and one of the major centers of global finance. The building contains the offices of the Swiss insurance company Swiss Re, which commissioned the project, as well as other office space for rental and a large number of shops. Its spectacular elongated shape and its circular ground plan offer aerodynamic benefits, such as reducing wind load and downdraughts. What's more, various technical measures provide natural ventilation and make the building far more energy-efficient than a conventional office block. Composed of a metal framework encased in an aluminum and glass façade, the whole structure is designed to convey natural light from the exterior to the center, thereby reducing the need for artificial lighting. At the top of the building, there is a panoramic private members' bar and restaurant, which offers a spectacular and unique 360-degree view over London. And at its foot, there is an accompanying plaza development with numerous cafés and restaurants.

NORDDEUTSCHE LANDESBANK
HANOVER, GERMANY

Following the wishes of the senior management of Norddeutsche Landesbank, this unique bank building incorporates a particularly well thought-out approach to sustainable development, with the objective of maximizing the comfort of its users.

The German agency Behnisch & Partners won a competition to design a simple service building, but the project grew to an unexpected scale when it was decided that it should become the head office for the bank and its 1,500 employees. Finished in 2002, the building takes up a whole block stretching between Hanover city center and a residential district. An outdoor courtyard divides the low-rise buildings around the edges of the plot from the stepped tower in the center. Fully glazed tubular footbridges link the different elements of the structure. This free-form architecture, with its diversity of shapes and irregular ground plans, brings the whole building down to a human scale. All the work spaces receive natural light and are of a comfortable size (120–160 square feet). On the ground floor there are numerous outdoor terraces, bars, and restaurants to enable employees to have a break at any point during the working day.

SOUTHERN CROSS RAILWAY STATION
MELBOURNE, AUSTRALIA

Compared by the architect to a sand dune, the rippling roof that covers this multi-transport station has helped to give a strong identity to the Melbourne business district in which it is situated.

Located near the docks, this architecturally striking station stands between Bourke Street and Collins Street, with its front façade taking up the whole block along Spencer Street. Completed in 2007, the building was produced by the British architect Sir Nicholas Grimshaw. It is notable for its vast, undulating roof, part of which is opaque, and part of which is glazed. The architect, wanting to maintain a visual continuity with the surrounding streets and the docks beyond, designed open or glazed façades in order not to obstruct views—thus the traveler can enjoy a high-angle view of the city while descending from the station's upper concourse to the platforms at street level. The station's management offices are housed in yellow compartments on stilts, with shops below. The curved lines of the roof were specially designed to facilitate the extraction of diesel fumes and hot air. This, along with the orientation of the building to make the most of prevailing winds, helps to keep the station at a comfortable temperature—a constant challenge in this part of the world.

This church, officially named Dio Padre Misericordioso, was commissioned by the curacy of Rome to commemorate the two thousandth anniversary of the birth of Christ.

Designed by the American architect Richard Meier and erected in 2003, the building stands in the suburbs of Rome, in the middle of the residential district of Tor Tre Teste. It is not just a church but also a community center. The structure is notable for its immaculate whiteness, a trademark of this architect, as well as for its three curved structures of varying heights, which stand side by side, symbolizing the Holy Trinity—the Father, the Son, and the Holy Spirit. These concrete "sails" define the interior space: the first two house the chapel and the baptistery, whereas the largest of the three delimits the main worshipping area of the church. The windows, which have been cleverly inset between these shells, let in floods of light and provide a subtle play of light and shadow. The way in which these curved structures are supported by the building's high, narrow, perpendicular wall demonstrates considerable technical skill. What's more, the concrete is self-cleaning, so it will never lose its whiteness.

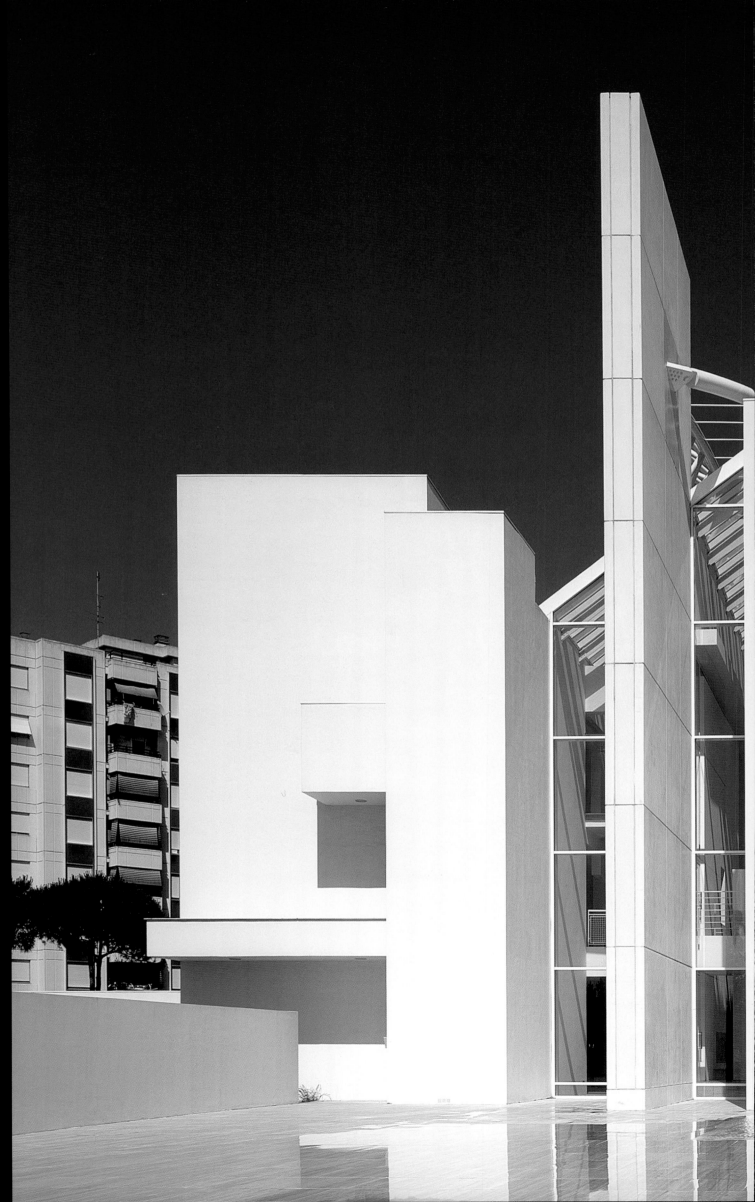

PHILHARMONIC HALL
LUXEMBOURG, LUXEMBOURG

Hosting more than 400 performances a year, this auditorium, also known as the Grande-Duchess Joséphine-Charlotte Concert Hall, is one of Europe's leading classical music venues.

Situated in the Plateau de Kirchberg, an administrative district to the northeast of the city center, and opened in 2005, the building was designed by Frenchman Christian de Portzamparc. It has a sophisticated style, much like this architect's other works. Measuring 420 by 358 feet, the building's ground plan is oval in shape, like an eye, with a curved façade made up of 823 narrow steel columns, each standing 66 feet high. These are painted white and form a colonnade around the 1,500-seat grand auditorium. Bathed in natural light, a long gangway functions both as a promenade and as a means of access to the various levels of the hall, in particular the eight towers of boxes, which are arranged uniformly around the stalls. Adjoining this imposing edifice is a petal-shaped construction, which houses a 313-seat chamber music hall.

NATIONAL GRAND THEATER
BEIJING, CHINA

Nicknamed the "Egg" by the people of Beijing, this architecturally bold cultural center has attracted controversy: some people love it, others loathe it.

Designed by the French architect Paul Andreu, the building was completed in 2007. It is located right in the historical center of Beijing, not far from Tiananmen Square and the Forbidden City. The idea behind the complex was that it should be a "city of theaters," a transparent island on an artificial lake surrounded by a new urban park. Pedestrians can reach it via underground passageways. The building comprises an opera house, a concert hall, two theaters, exhibition spaces, restaurants, and shops. This bulbous, glass- and titanium-covered shell measures 695 by 472 feet. At night, the National Grand Theater lights the sky through its glass walls and seems to float on the artificial lake that surrounds it and over which it towers by 151 feet. This curved shape, slightly concave at the center, was inspired by the traditional Chinese symbols of yin and yang, with the two-tone patterning on the shell evoking these two complementary elements. This design is also reminiscent of a safety curtain opening at the start of a performance.

NATIONAL STADIUM
BEIJING, CHINA

Nicknamed the "Bird's Nest" by the Chinese, who immediately took it to their hearts, this stadium was inaugurated during the opening ceremony of the 2008 Beijing Summer Olympics.

The stadium, designed by the Swiss agency Herzog & de Meuron, is located in the Olympic Park, to the north of the Forbidden City. The architects, assisted by the artist Ai Weiwei, were inspired by Chinese ceramics. The base of the stadium is angled slightly, which makes its northern and southern stands higher than its eastern and western stands. This required a considerable number of steel supports—more than 46,000 tons of the metal went into the construction. Originally, the stadium was to have been covered by a gigantic retractable roof, but this plan was abandoned on the grounds of cost. As in most Herzog & de Meuron projects, color has been used sparingly. However, the outside of the arena and terracing are in a typically Chinese red lacquer and the interior elements are in matte black. In terms of formal and technological innovation, this building is one of the boldest constructions in contemporary world architecture.

This head office of a Japanese TV channel is a particularly innovative form of its genre.

The visionary Japanese architect Kenzo Tange completed this imposing 25-story building in 1997, and it immediately became the defining feature of the artificial island of Odaiba in Tokyo Bay. Composed of two partly hollowed-out blocks, which are connected by covered gangways and external elevators, the building is clad in titanium, making it shimmer in the sun. The façade is paced by a grid pattern made up of columns and set-back openings. A huge sphere, also encased in titanium, has been positioned at the top, where it houses an observation deck and a restaurant. With a diameter of 105 feet and a weight of 1,200 tons, this UFO-like structure gives the building an undeniably futuristic appeal. The covered escalators that protrude from the lower part of the façade are reminiscent of those at the Centre Pompidou in Paris.

**This building—
Frank Gehry's first
completed project in
New York—is without
doubt the world's
most architecturally
interesting office block.**

Built in 2007 in the
Chelsea district of
New York, the building
was commissioned by
the American media
group InterActivCorp to
accommodate 500 of
its employees. It has two
main sections: the lower
part, consisting of five
stories, is aligned with
the street, whereas the
upper part is set back all
the way around, creating
a continuous terrace.
Appearing as pliable as
a piece of folded white
paper, the building's
façade is entirely in glass,
distinguishing it from
Gehry's other works, which
tend to be clad in steel
and titanium. Here he has
used a concrete framework
covered in curved-glass
panels. The glass has
been fritted, a process
involving screen-printing
white ceramic dots onto
its surface. The dots vary
in concentration, creating
gradations between
opaque and clear areas in
such a way as to protect
the building's occupants
both from prying eyes and
strong sunlight. Among
the project's other unusual
features is its ground floor,
which—unlike most other
office blocks—doesn't
contain retail units opening
onto the street, but instead
consists of a vast hall.

MARINA BAY SANDS
SINGAPORE, SINGAPORE

Built on an overhang 650 feet above the ground, a spectacular "vanishing-edge or infinity" swimming pool offers an exceptional view over the city; it is by far the most stunning element of this project.

Completed in 2010, the seafront hotel complex Marina Bay Sands demonstrates an unprecedented level of ambition. Designed by the American architect Moshe Safdie, the development is laid out on a 37-acre site, which features a series of gardens, a seafront promenade, and wide pedestrianized avenues. Standing 640 feet tall, the building consists of three towers topped off with a 2.5-acre cantilevered structure called the "Sands Skypark." The "Sands Skypark" provides a host of amenities, including an observation deck, sumptuous gardens, a jogging track, and a 495-foot swimming pool. This hanging garden is planted with all manner of trees and shrubs. As well as its 2,560 luxury rooms, the hotel contains a conference center, numerous shops and restaurants, theaters, an art and science museum, a casino, and a nightclub. The architect had this to say about Marina Bay Sands: "It's really more than a project—it's a microcosm of a city and it was important to root it in Singapore's history, culture, and contemporary life."

JEWISH MUSEUM
BERLIN, GERMANY

Designed to disorientate the visitor, this strange, unsettling museum, nicknamed the "Blitz" by Berliners, has played host to more than five million people since it opened.

Opened without exhibits in 1998, then filled and officially opened in 2001, this was the project that made the name of its creator, the Polish–American architect Daniel Libeskind. It would take him ten years to produce the museum, which is devoted to the social, political, and cultural history of the Jewish inhabitants of Germany from the 14th century to the present day. Located in the heart of Berlin, on Lindenstraße, the building is set back from the street, leaving a large empty space laid out as a garden, designed to convey a feeling of absence. Its zigzag ground plan of broken lines represents a deconstructed Star of David. The riveted-zinc façade has been slashed with narrow openings, which project shards of light into the interior. The cramped, broken-up spaces convey a sense of unease and desolation—an effect that was intended by the architect, who had a particular stake in this project, having himself lost members of his family in the Holocaust.

DENVER ART MUSEUM
DENVER, USA

This prismatic construction, which astonishes with its jagged, menacing appearance, was inspired by the geology of the Rocky Mountains.

Situated right in the heart of Denver's new cultural quarter, this building (officially, the Frederic C. Hamilton Building) was designed by Daniel Libeskind. It is an extension of the existing art museum, which had already been enlarged in 1971 by the Italian Gio Ponti. Intended to house collections of modern and contemporary art, as well as works from Africa and Oceania, the extension increases the capacity of the existing museum by 40 percent. The long, pointed structure that juts out into open air, by far the most spectacular element of the building, consists of a reinforced concrete framework covered in glass and titanium panels. Visitors enter a vast, four-story atrium, brightly lit from above, then climb a staircase that tapers toward the exhibition galleries. All the interior walls are at an angle, so the curators had to install vertical picture rails to display the artworks. The unnerving-looking windows that have been gashed out of the façade convey natural light into the interior.

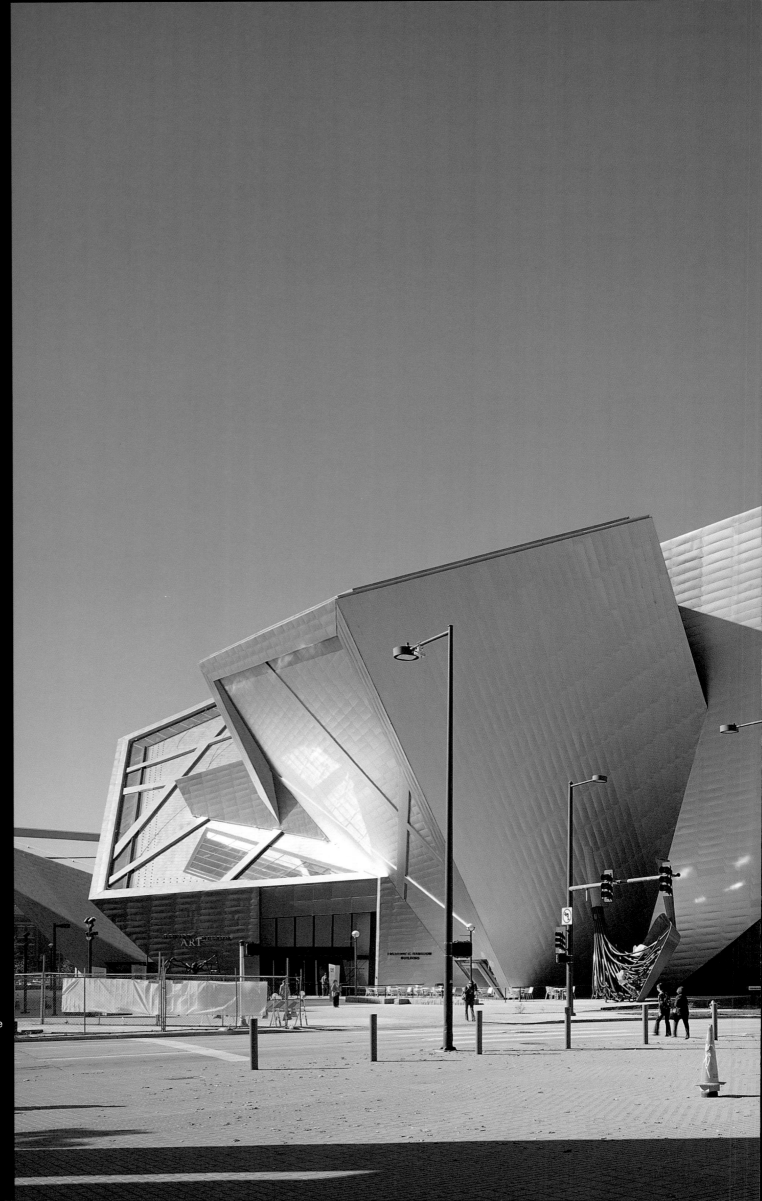

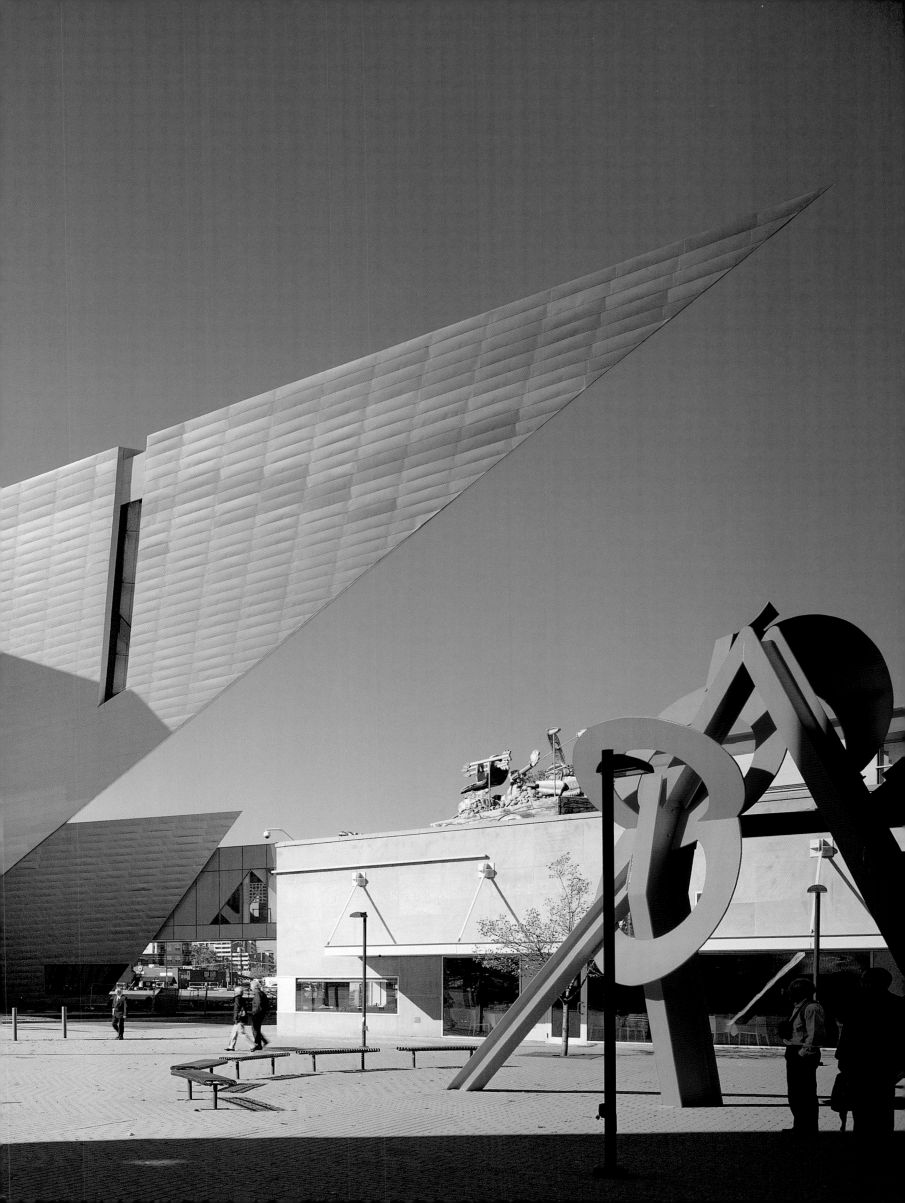

Resembling a circus big top, this museum, complete with its gardens and piazza, was inspired by a fabric-covered, woven-bamboo Chinese hat that its Japanese co-designer found one day in a Paris craft shop.

The Japanese and French architects Shigeru Ban and Jean de Gastines worked together to produce this highly technical building, which opened its doors to the public in 2010. It is an offshoot of the original Centre Pompidou in Paris, produced in 1977 by Renzo Piano and Richard Rogers. The roof design is notable for its double-curvature structure, which is supported by just a central 253-foot metal spire and four cone-shaped pillars around the edge of the building. The 86,000-square foot expanse of roofing is constructed of a glue-laminated timber lattice, strong enough to span 130 feet, which means that there is no need for pillars in the central nave, where the largest and most important works of art are displayed. The wooden framework is covered in a weatherproof fiberglass and Teflon (PTFE) membrane. In addition to the main nave, three galleries made of rectangular tubes of reinforced concrete criss-cross one on top of the other beneath the roof. Their glazed openings at each end provide views over the cathedral, the railway station, and the Parc de la Seille.

PHILOLOGICAL LIBRARY
BERLIN, GERMANY

Informally known as the "Berlin Brain," this library is particularly striking at night when its interior lighting reveals the checkerboard structure of its exterior, alternating between opacity and transparency.

The British agency Foster + Partners was commissioned by the Free University of Berlin—one of the city's major academic institutions since the Second World War—to renovate its 1970s building stock and to construct a library for the Faculty of Philology. Finished in 2005, this four-story building consists of an enormous dome built on a site created by joining together six of the university's courtyards. Its radial steel framework supports an aluminum- and glass-paneled enclosure. An inner membrane made of translucent glass fiber filters the daylight. This double envelope creates natural ventilation and acts as a heat shield. The library has a capacity of 650 work spaces and houses a major collection of 700,000 books. The interior spaces follow the curves of the exterior, and the restrained quality of the light provides students with optimal conditions for study and concentration.

ATIONAL ART CENTER
OKYO, JAPAN

his enormous building, otable for its opulent, orrugated-glass façade, s the largest museum n Japan.

uilt in 2006, this art enter was conceived by he Japanese architect isho Kurokawa. Located n the high-end shopping istrict of Roppongi, in the eart of the downtown, the useum occupies land elonging to the University f Tokyo. Essentially, the uilding is a simple cuboid, vith a structure made out f concrete. However, s main façade, which boks onto a tree-planted laza, is strikingly different. Consisting of an immense lass wave, which rolls cross the full width of he building, it houses gigantic atrium. Glass ouvers shelter the atrium rom the sun's rays. Upon ntering the building via steel-and-glass cone, isitors pass by another wo larger cones—these nes are upturned, nade of concrete, and opped with a café and restaurant respectively. nside, the center oasts an impressive 50,000 square feet of xhibition space, a library, n auditorium, and a useum store. Visitors re also able to access rooftop garden. The useum does not have permanent collection; nstead the various alleries display numerous emporary exhibitions—from contemporary works by apanese artists to visiting howcases of some of the vorld's great works of art.

FREITAG SHOP
ZURICH, SWITZERLAND

Produced from recycled materials, this "bonsai skyscraper," as some people have described it, clearly ushers in a new generation of eco-buildings.

Founded in 1993, the Zurich-based Freitag brand, specializing in handbags made from recycled materials, enlisted the young Swiss agency Spillmann Echsle Architekten to design their first flagship store in the city. Completed in 2006, the building is situated on Geroldstraße in the very fashionable Zurich West district. Standing 85 feet tall, it is made entirely from disused freight containers, which were transported directly to the site by rail from the port of Hamburg. The containers were stacked and attached to each other using fastenings salvaged from the shipping industry. The asymmetric structure consists of four stacks of containers side by side, the tallest of which is nine containers high. The four-container stack on the far right has been given over to the shop itself, where more than 1,500 bags are on display. The four floors are connected by a metal staircase in the center of the building. At the top of the main tower is an observation deck, which offers extraordinary views over the city, the surrounding roads, the lake, and the mountains in the distance.

GATESHEAD MILLENNIUM BRIDGE
NEWCASTLE, UK

Conceived as a millennium project, this bridge is illuminated at night with arcs of light that reflect in the river. Ingenious as well as beautiful, it has a tilting mechanism to let ships pass under it.

Officially opened by Queen Elizabeth II on 7 May 2002, this tilt bridge is the work of the British architects WilkinsonEyre. Located in northeast England, the bridge crosses the Tyne, linking the city of Newcastle to a new arts complex in Gateshead, and it has made a major contribution to the region's revival. With a span of 344 feet, the structure consists of two graceful arches, one forming the deck and the other its support. Its unique tilt mechanism has a hydraulic operation that lifts the deck by 82 feet in just four and a half minutes, thereby letting ships pass with minimal disruption to the pedestrians and cyclists who use the bridge. The structure was assembled off site and installed in one piece using one of the world's largest floating cranes. This remarkable engineering project has received numerous awards, including the prestigious Stirling Prize for Architecture in 2002.

XPERIENCE MUSIC ROJECT
ATTLE, USA

cated within the eattle Center cultural mplex, this building is spired by the Fender ratocaster—a type of uitar that the American ck star (and Seattle tive) Jimi Hendrix ed to enjoy smashing in concert.

e flamboyant architect ank Gehry produced is building, which ened in 2000. The ilding is dedicated to merican popular music d was commissioned the billionaire Paul len, co-founder of icrosoft. To give the ucture its particularly mplex curvilinear yle, the architect ade use of computer ftware designed for the rospace industry. The ter layer is made up of re than 3,000 aluminum d steel panels, which m seven multi-faceted ells that reflect the light d sparkle under the sun. ables drawn over the çade are reminiscent of oken guitar strings. The erior and the exterior veal a variety of colors— otably purple, in a nod Hendrix's classic song urple Haze." Besides aying tribute to Jimi endrix, one of the most eative and influential merican musicians of his a, the building houses re than 80,000 artifacts m rock history, exhibition aces, a restaurant, a okstore, and offices.

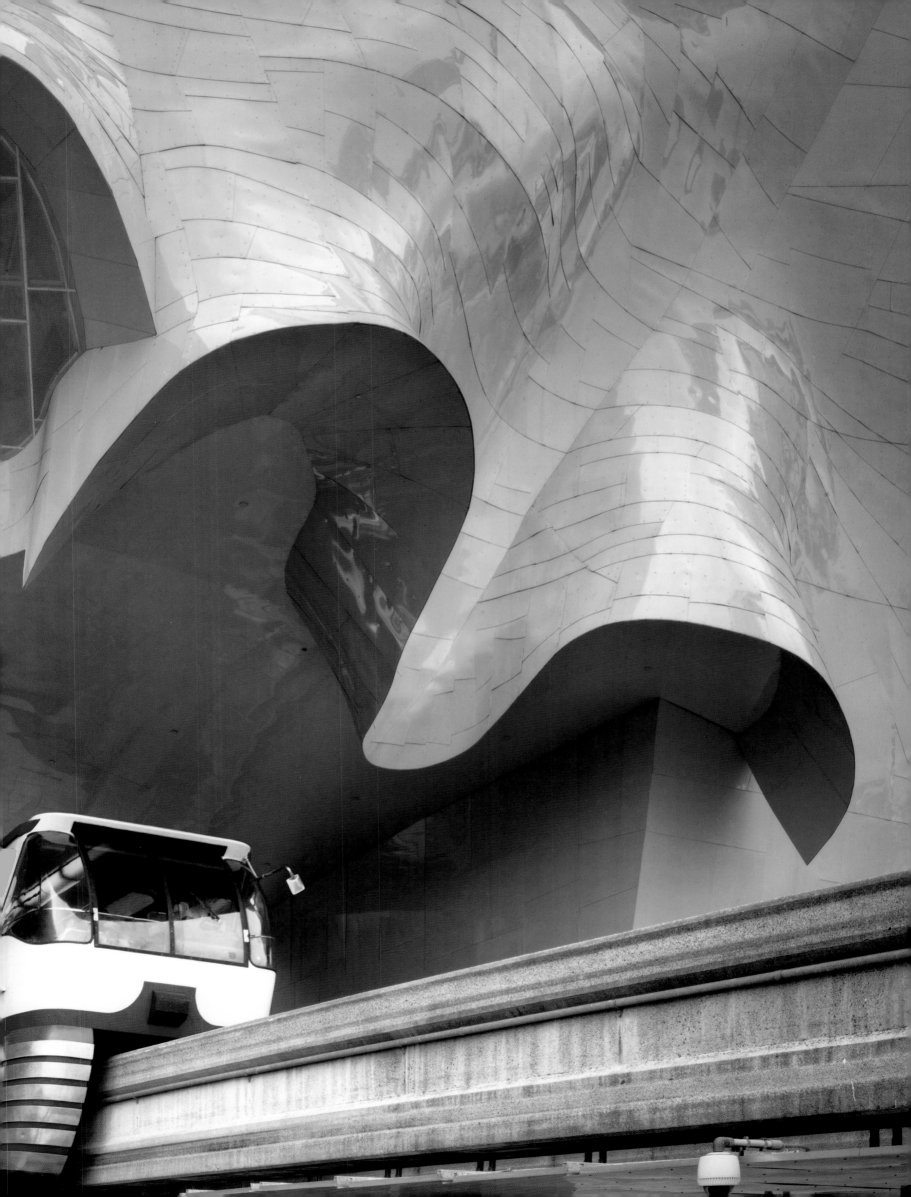

CHANEL MOBILE ART PAVILION
PARIS, FRANCE

A luxury showcase, this globe-trotting mobile pavilion was commissioned by the fashion designer Karl Lagerfeld to enhance the Chanel brand and one of its most famous creations in particular, the quilted handbag.

Designed by Zaha Hadid and launched in 2008, this traveling exhibition space is immediately recognizable by its organic, futuristic shell. Easily transportable by container, the pavilion has visited cities such as Hong Kong, Tokyo, New York, Los Angeles, London, and Moscow to exhibit works by 15 contemporary artists, all inspired by the iconic quilted Chanel bag. The structure measures 95 by 148 feet and consists of a series of metal arches laid out around an inner courtyard. The whole thing is covered in a skin made of panels of fiber-reinforced plastic (FRP). The curved folds on some parts of the membrane create the bizarre effect of the structure having been crumpled. The architect has come up with a fluid space, with smooth transitions. Light is used to bring the interior to life: artificial lighting built into the floor washes up against the walls and emphasizes their contours; and this is complemented by natural light entering overhead through the translucent ETFE ceiling. In 2011, Chanel donated the pavilion to the Institut du Monde Arabe (Arab World Institute) in Paris, where it now resides permanently.

UNDERCOVER LAB
TOKYO, JAPAN

Made from glass, corrugated iron and bricks imported from London, this mysterious building functions as a showcase for the Japanese couturier Jun Takahashi, a designer renowned for his innovative, avant-garde style and his punk sensibility.

The building was designed for Takahashi by the Anglo-Italian architects Klein and Dytham, who set up business in Japan in 1991, and it reflects Takahashi's love of urban culture. Completed in 2001, Undercover Lab (in which the word "undercover" has both literal and figurative connotations) is hidden away in the depths of an alleyway in the lively Harajuku district of Tokyo. The couturier wanted the building to be so unassuming that it would disappear into its surroundings, an effect that the architects have achieved in a particularly original way. The project consists of three elements: a brick-built studio on three levels, a fully glazed stair- and lift-shaft, and a 72-foot long cantilevered showroom. Standing 33 feet above ground level, this black corrugated-iron box is reminiscent of a shipping container. The area created below serves both as car park and circulation space. The long, narrow interior of the showroom is ideal for presenting new collections, thanks above all to its 66-foot long display rail.

CONTEMPORARY ART MUSEUM
NITERÓI, BRAZIL

Although modest in size, this museum is world famous for its flying-saucer shape balanced on the edge of a cliff over the bay of Rio de Janeiro.

Now more than 100 years old, and with a career of more than 70 years behind him, the architect Oscar Niemeyer is known for organic, sensual shapes in immaculate white concrete. Designed for his native country and opened in 1996, this museum of contemporary art surprised many with its futuristic form—a UFO-like dome placed on top of a 30-foot high central cylinder and accessible via a separate spiral gangway. The structure comprises three levels, which fan out to a diameter of 165 feet. These fully glazed floors offer a stunning view over Guanabara Bay and the famous Sugarloaf Mountain. They also house a collection of more than 1,000 works of art of the highest order. The building is reflected in a mirror-pool at its base. A vast esplanade occupies the surrounding area, opening up a clear view of this "spaceship-museum," which has become the most famous and popular building in Brazil.

BURJ AL ARAB
DUBAI, UNITED ARAB EMIRATES

With a name meaning "Tower of the Arabs" in Arabic, this building is the most luxurious hotel in the world—it has seven stars—but it is also the most expensive, with rates of up to 4,000 US Dollars a night!

Produced by the young British architect Tom Wright, the tower welcomed its first guests in 1999. He intended it to become the city's symbol, much like the Opera House is to Sydney or the Eiffel Tower is to Paris. In order to maximize the effect of its spectacular height (1,053 feet) and its unique shape, that of a sail billowing in the wind, the architect decided that the hotel should be built on an artificial island so that it would be reflected in the sea. In terms of construction, the tower is in concrete, with a glass façade. The sea-facing part of the atrium façade has been coated in Teflon to protect it from gusts of sand. At almost 600 feet, the atrium is currently the tallest in the world. The roof of the building features a heliport, tennis courts, and a dramatic panoramic restaurant suspended in mid-air by means of an 89-foot cantilever. The hotel boasts 202 suites, ranging in size from 1,800 square feet to an absolutely mind-boggling 8,400 square feet.

GUGGENHEIM MUSEUM
BILBAO, SPAIN

This museum has become one of the most highly regarded late 20th-century buildings in the world, welcoming a million visitors each year. The significant economic benefit it has brought the city of Bilbao has been christened the "Guggenheim effect."

Located in Bilbao, in the Spanish Basque Country, the Guggenheim Museum—the fourth of its kind in the world—houses a major collection of post-war and contemporary modern art. Designed by Frank Gehry, its doors were opened to the public in 1997. Now thoroughly enmeshed in the urban and cultural fabric of Bilbao, the building is notable for its curvilinear forms. It is composed of a series of interconnected elements—some are geometric in form and clad in limestone, others are more organic and covered in a metallic skin made from titanium panels, on which the sunlight plays throughout the day. The museum includes exhibition spaces, a 300-seat auditorium, a restaurant, two cafés, and a gift shop/bookstore. The Bilbao Guggenheim is the most important example of the deconstructivist style adopted in the 1990s by architects such as Daniel Libeskind, Bernard Tschumi, and Zaha Hadid.

INDEXOFARCHITECTS

FURTHERREADING

This list contains books and articles on the major figures of contemporary architecture. There are also more specialized works for those who wish to focus on specific themes.

Alba, Roberto de. *Paul Rudolph: The Late Work*. New York: Princeton Architectural Press, 2003.

Àlvarez Garreta, Ariadna. *Skyscrapers*. Mexico, New York, Barcelona: Atrium, 2002.

Asensio, Francisco (ed.). *Rem Koolhaas/OMA*. Düsseldorf: teNeues, 2002.

Asensio, Francisco. *New Architecture: An International Atlas*. New York: Abrams, 2007.

Barreneche, Raul A. *New Museums*. London: Phaidon Press, 2005.

Barreneche, Raul A. *New Retail*. London: Phaidon Press, 2008.

Béret, Chantal (ed.). *Jean Nouvel*. Paris: éditions du Centre Georges Pompidou, 2002.

Bognar, Botond. *Hiroshi Hara: The "Floating World" of his Architecture*. New York: Wiley & Sons, 2001.

Bruggen, Coosje van. *Frank O. Gehry: Guggenheim Museum, Bilbao*. New York: Abrams, 1998.

Casamonti, Marco. *Jean Nouvel*. Milan: Motta Architettura, 2009.

Celant, Germano. *Frank O. Gehry: Since 1997*. Milan: Skira, 2009.

Dal Co, Francesco. *Tadao Ando, 1995-2010*. New York: Prestel, 2010.

El Croquis. *Frank Gehry, 1987-2003*. Madrid: El Croquis, 2006.

Futagawa, Yukio (ed.). *"Hiroshi Hara", GA Architect, no.13*. Tokyo: ADA Edita, 1993.

Futagawa, Yukio (ed.). *"Toyo Ito, 1970-2001", GA Architect, no.17*. Tokyo: ADA Edita, 2001.

Futagawa, Yukio. *Zaha Hadid: Recent Project*. Tokyo: ADA Edita, 2010.

Guccione, Margherita. *Zaha Hadid*. Milan: Motta Architettura, 2007.

Irving, Mark. *1001 Buildings You Must See Before You Die*. London: Quintessence, 2007.

Jodidio, Philip. *Calatrava: Complete Works, 1979-2009*. Cologne: Taschen, 2009.

Migayrou, Frédéric. *Morphosis: Continuities of the Incomplete*. Paris: éditions du Centre Georges Pompidou, 2008.

Phaidon. *The Phaidon Atlas of Contemporary World Architecture*. London: Phaidon Press, 2004.

Phaidon. *The Phaidon Atlas of 21st Century World Architecture*. London: Phaidon Press, 2008.

Piano, Renzo. *On Tour With Renzo Piano*. London: Phaidon Press, 2004.

Tzonis, Alexander. *Santiago Calatrava: The Complete Works*. New York: Rizzoli, 2004.

Weisman Art Museum. *The Building: Weisman Art Museum, Frank Gehry Designs*. Minneapolis: University of Minnesota Press, 2003.

Yoshida, Nobuyuki (ed.). *"Herzog & de Meuron, 2002-2006", A+U, Architecture and Urbanism, special issue no.8*. Tokyo: A+U Publishing Co., 2006.

CHRONOLOGY

PICTURECREDITS